BEANSTALK'S BASICS FOR
PIANO

THEORY BOOK
LEVEL 2

BY CHERYL FINN

ISBN 978-0-87718-046-3

WILLIS MUSIC

EXCLUSIVELY DISTRIBUTED BY

HAL•LEONARD®

Visit Hal Leonard Online at
www.halleonard.com

World headquarters, contact:
Hal Leonard
7777 West Bluemound Road
Milwaukee, WI 53213
Email: info@halleonard.com

In Europe, contact:
Hal Leonard Europe Limited
42 Wigmore Street
Marylebone, London, W1U 2RN
Email: info@halleonardeurope.com

In Australia, contact:
Hal Leonard Australia Pty. Ltd.
4 Lentara Court
Cheltenham, Victoria, 3192 Australia
Email: info@halleonard.com.au

CONTENTS

A NOTE TO PARENTS AND TEACHERS

The study of music theory is essential to the development of the young musician. Not only does this study help to expand upon the concepts taught at the piano lesson, but it also gives the student a greater understanding and appreciation of the wonder that is music.

The Beanstalk series was designed to be used with colorful, attractive stickers that reward a job well done. The student may receive stickers for note-naming and note-writing drills, for ear training, and sight-reading exercises, and for successfully completing review pages. These exclusive stickers are available for download using the unique code found on the title page of this book and may be printed using Avery Round Labels (6450), available at Avery.com and other online retailers.

Each theory page corresponds directly with material covered in **Beanstalk's Basics for Piano**. The student progresses gradually, in a logical fashion and continually builds on concepts previously learned.

Beanstalk's Basics for Piano Theory also features a further learning tool called **Thinking Cap**. **Thinking Cap** challenges the student to search for answers to one or more theoretical questions and to provide these answers verbally as part of a musical dialogue. This fun exercise encourages students to carefully consider and discuss new concepts as they arise.

We wish much success to all students as they strive to expand their musical horizons!

To Alanna and Brianne

A NEW RHYTHM

A **QUARTER NOTE** is equal in length to **TWO** eighth notes:

A dot placed after a note makes that note longer by half its value.
A **DOTTED QUARTER NOTE** is equal to **THREE** eighth notes:

A **DOTTED QUARTER NOTE** is usually followed by
an eighth note and is counted like this:

1 + 2 +

Example:

1 + 2 + 3 + 4 +   1 + 2 + 3 + 4 +   1 + 2 + 3 + 4 +   1 + 2 + 3 + 4 +

1. Write the counts and add bar lines to the following. Clap the rhythm and count out loud.

CORRESPONDS WITH PAGES 5 & 6 OF BEANSTALK'S LESSON BOOK 2.

2. Write the counts and add bar lines to the following. Clap the rhythm and count out loud.

FOR THE TEACHER:

CORRESPONDS WITH PAGES 5 & 6 OF BEANSTALK'S LESSON BOOK 2.

INTRODUCING 6THS

An interval of a 6th is written **LINE** to **SPACE** or **SPACE** to **LINE**:

THINKING CAP

What is a 6th higher than F?
What is a 6th lower than G?

For each of the following write the note which is a 6th **ABOVE**. Use whole notes.

For each of the following write the note which is a 6th **BELOW**. Use whole notes.

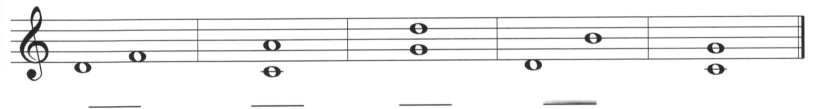

Name the following intervals.

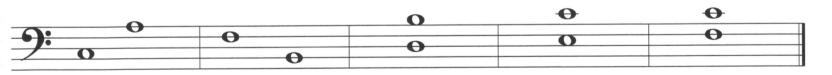

NOW HEAR THIS!

Your teacher will play a series of 6ths. Close your eyes and listen. Is each of the 6ths ABOVE or BELOW the given note?

FOR THE TEACHER:

INTERVAL REVIEW

Name the following intervals.

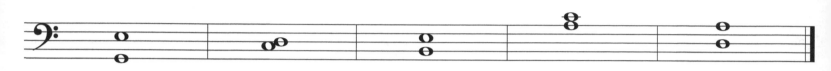

____   ____   ____   ____   ____

____   ____   ____   ____   ____

HARMONIC OR MELODIC?

THINKING CAP

What **KIND** of intervals are these? Put an **'H'** below each **HARMONIC** interval and an 'M' below each **MELODIC** interval.

How can you tell if an interval is **HARMONIC** or **MELODIC**?

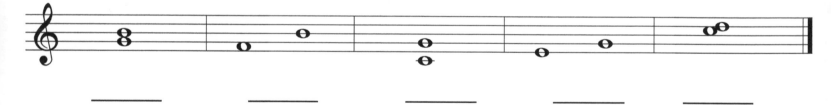

____   ____   ____   ____   ____

____   ____   ____   ____   ____

NOW HEAR THIS!

Your teacher will play a series of intervals. Close your eyes and listen Are the intervals **HARMONIC** or **MELODIC**?

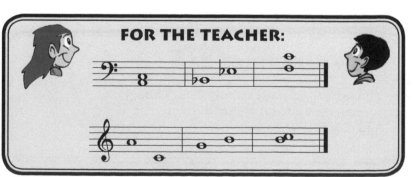

FOR THE TEACHER:

CORRESPONDS WITH PAGE 8 OF BEANSTALK'S LESSON BOOK 2.

NOTE WRITING

Write the following notes in the **BASS** clef. Use whole notes.

| Middle C | E Flat | B | A | F Sharp |

Write the following notes in the **TREBLE** clef. Use half notes. (Remember to adjust the stems.)

| E Natural | D | C Sharp | G | B Flat |

Write the following notes in the **BASS** clef. Use quarter notes.

| D | G Sharp | C | E | A Flat |

Write the following notes in the **TREBLE** clef. Use dotted half notes.

| Middle C | B | G Natural | D | F Sharp |

Write the following notes in the **BASS** clef. Use single eighth notes.

| E | G | D Flat | F | A |

Write the following notes in the **TREBLE** clef. Use dotted quarter notes.

| F Sharp | F Natural | D | G | E Flat |

CORRESPONDS WITH PAGE 9 OF BEANSTALK'S LESSON BOOK 2.

NOTE NAMING

A NEW NOTE:
E

IT'S NICK!

Time yourself naming the following notes on the grand staff.
(Remember to check the key signature!) Add stems to make half notes.

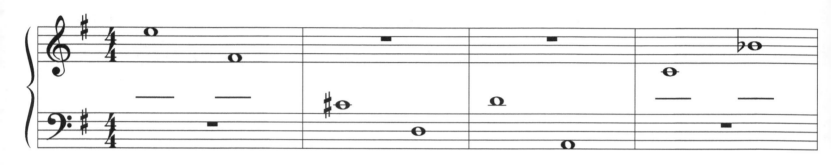

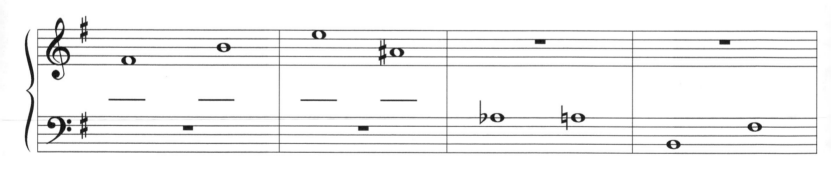

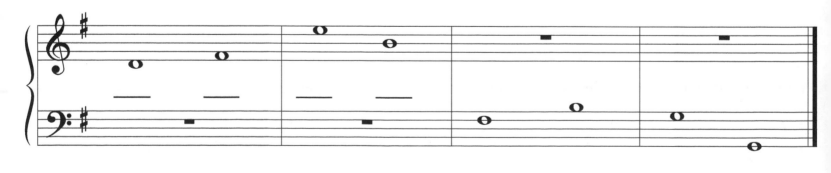

I named these notes in _____ minutes and _____ seconds!

CORRESPONDS WITH PAGE 10 OF BEANSTALK'S LESSON BOOK 2.

MORE NOTE NAMING

A NEW NOTE:

F

THINKING CAP

Will the stem go up
or down on the new 'F'?

Name the following notes. Add stems and dots to make dotted half notes.

SECRET MELODY!

1. Sight read the following.
2. Name the **SECRET MELODY**!
3. Fill in the note names.

SIGHT READING

_____

(TITLE)

TRADITIONAL

CORRESPONDS WITH PAGES 11 & 12 OF BEANSTALK'S LESSON BOOK 2.

INTRODUCING 7THS

The interval of a 7th is written **SPACE** to **SPACE** or **LINE** to **LINE**:

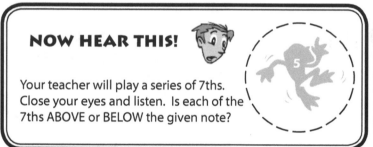

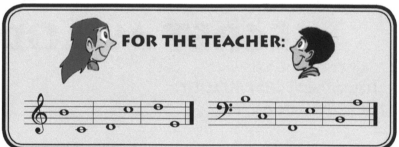

THINKING CAP

What is a 7th above A?
What is a 7th below B?

For each of the following write the note which is a 7th **ABOVE**. Use whole notes.

For each of the following write the note which is a 7th **BELOW**. Use whole notes.

NOW HEAR THIS!

Your teacher will play a series of 7ths.
Close your eyes and listen. Is each of the
7ths ABOVE or BELOW the given note?

FOR THE TEACHER:

PUZZLE FUN!

Find the secret composer. Fill in the blanks with the correct Italian terms.

WORD BANK: ALLEGRETTO LENTO MODERATO CANTABILE RITARDANDO GRAZIOSO

1. This word means to play at a **MODERATE** speed.

2. This word means to play **SLOWLY**.

3. This word means to play **GRACEFULLY**.

4. This word means to play in a **SINGING STYLE**.

5. This word means to play **GRADUALLY SLOWER**.

6. This word means to play **QUICKLY,**
   but not as quickly as allegro.

The secret composer is: ___ ___ ___ ___ ___ ___
                        1. 2. 3. 4. 5. 6.

CORRESPONDS WITH PAGE 13 OF BEANSTALK'S LESSON BOOK 2.

SEMITONES

A **SEMITONE** or **HALF STEP** is the closest distance there is between **TWO** keys.

THINKING CAP

What key is a semitone higher than F sharp?

Draw an arrow to the key which is a **SEMITONE** higher than the key marked with an **X**.

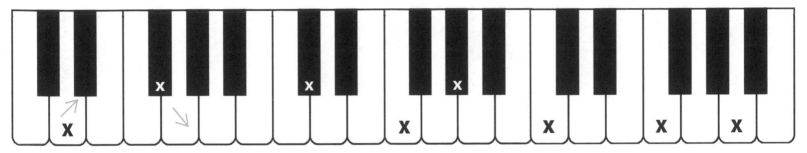

Draw an arrow to the key which is a **SEMITONE** lower than the key marked with an **X**.

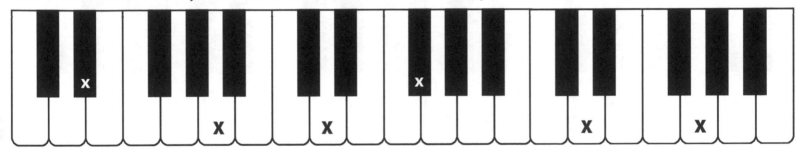

Most semitones occur between a black and white key, or a white and black key **EXCEPT** between **B** and **C** and **E** and **F**. Because there is no black key between these keys, these semitones occur between two white keys.

THINKING CAP

What key is a semitone higher than E?

Draw an arrow to the key which is a **SEMITONE** higher than the key marked with an **X**.

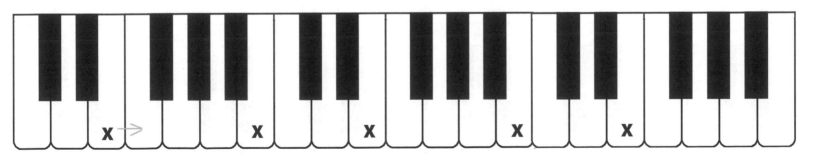

Draw an arrow to the key which is a **SEMITONE** lower than the key marked with an **X**.

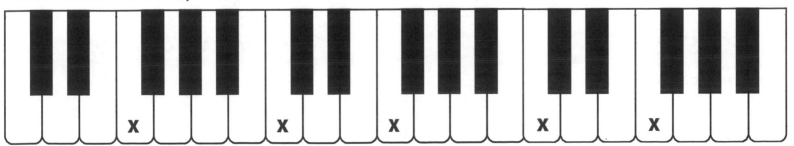

CORRESPONDS WITH PAGE 14 OF BEANSTALK'S LESSON BOOK 2.

WHOLE TONES

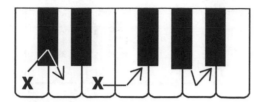

A **WHOLE TONE** or **WHOLE STEP** is made up of **TWO** semitones. Notice there is always a key in between.

THINKING CAP

What key is a whole tone higher than G?

Draw an arrow to the key which is a **WHOLE TONE** higher than the key marked with an **X**.

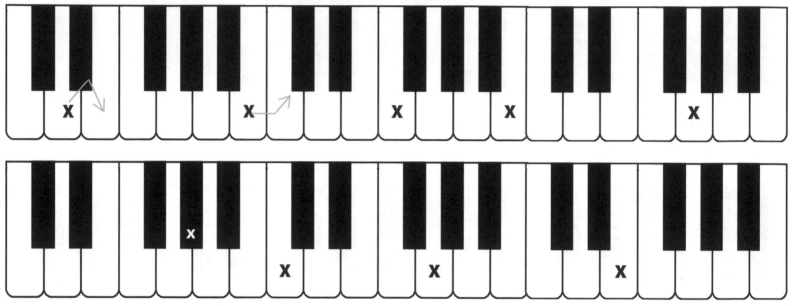

Draw an arrow to the key which is a **WHOLE TONE** lower than the key marked with an **X**.

THINKING CAP

What key is a whole tone lower than B flat?

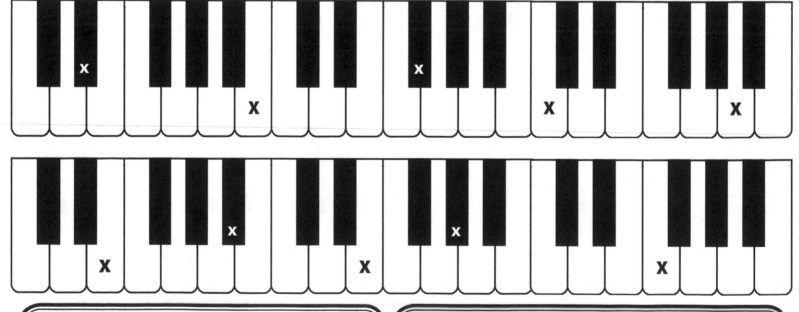

NOW HEAR THIS!

Your teacher will play a series of **SEMITONES** and **WHOLE TONES**. Close your eyes and listen. Can you identify which are walking UP and which are walking **DOWN**.

FOR THE TEACHER:

CORRESPONDS WITH PAGE 14 OF BEANSTALK'S LESSON BOOK 2.

TETRACHORDS

A **TETRACHORD** is a series of **FOUR** notes which follow this pattern:

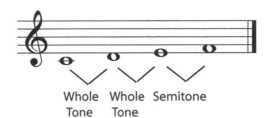

Whole Tone   Whole Tone   Semitone

THINKING CAP

Name the notes of a tetrachord beginning on G.

On the lines below each of the following tetrachords, write **WT** for **WHOLE TONE** or **ST** for **SEMITONE**. (The first one has been done for you as an example.) When you have finished, play each tetrachord.

Tetrachord beginning on C:

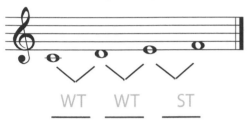

WT   WT   ST

Tetrachord beginning on G:

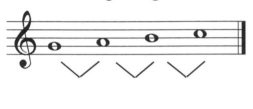

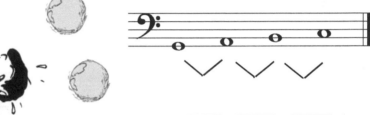

Tetrachord beginning on F:

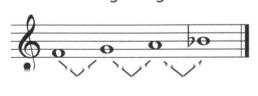

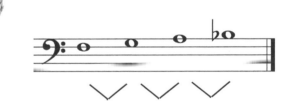

Tetrachord beginning on D:

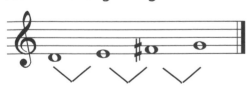

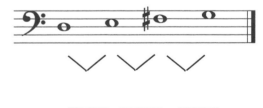

Tetrachord beginning on A:

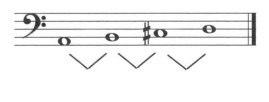

CORRESPONDS WITH PAGE 15 OF BEANSTALK'S LESSON BOOK 2.

SCALES

Every major scale is made up of **TWO TETRACHORDS** which are connected by a **WHOLE TONE**.

The pattern for a **MAJOR SCALE** is:

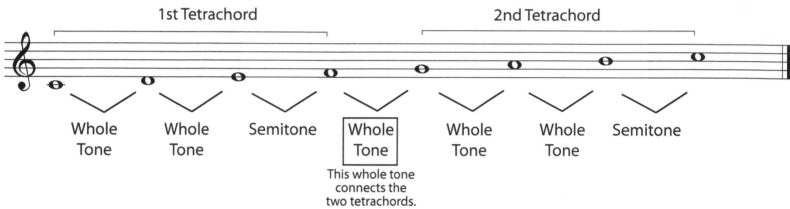

1st Tetrachord				2nd Tetrachord		
Whole Tone	Whole Tone	Semitone	Whole Tone	Whole Tone	Whole Tone	Semitone

This whole tone connects the two tetrachords.

For the following **MAJOR SCALES**, write **WT** below each **WHOLE TONE** and **ST** below each **SEMITONE**. Mark both tetrachords. (The first one has been done for you as an example.)

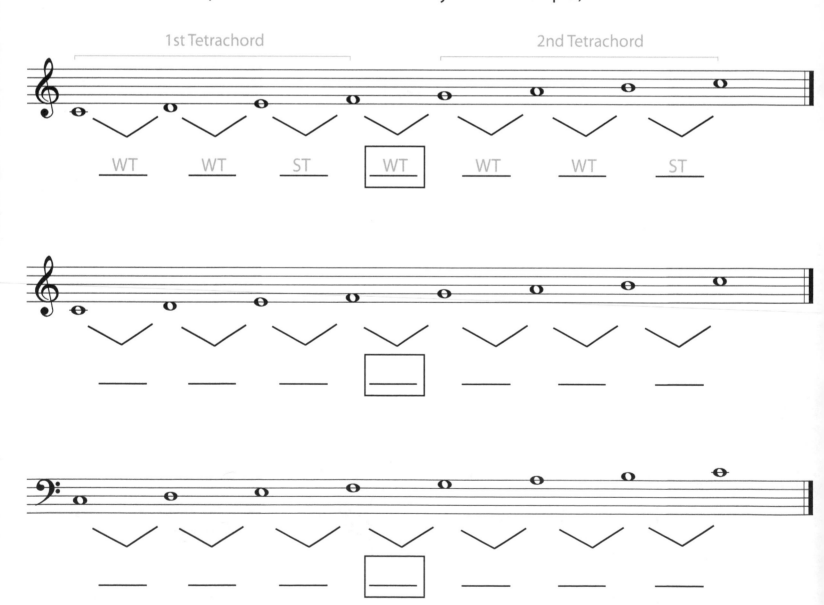

CORRESPONDS WITH PAGES 16 & 17 OF BEANSTALK'S LESSON BOOK 2.

14

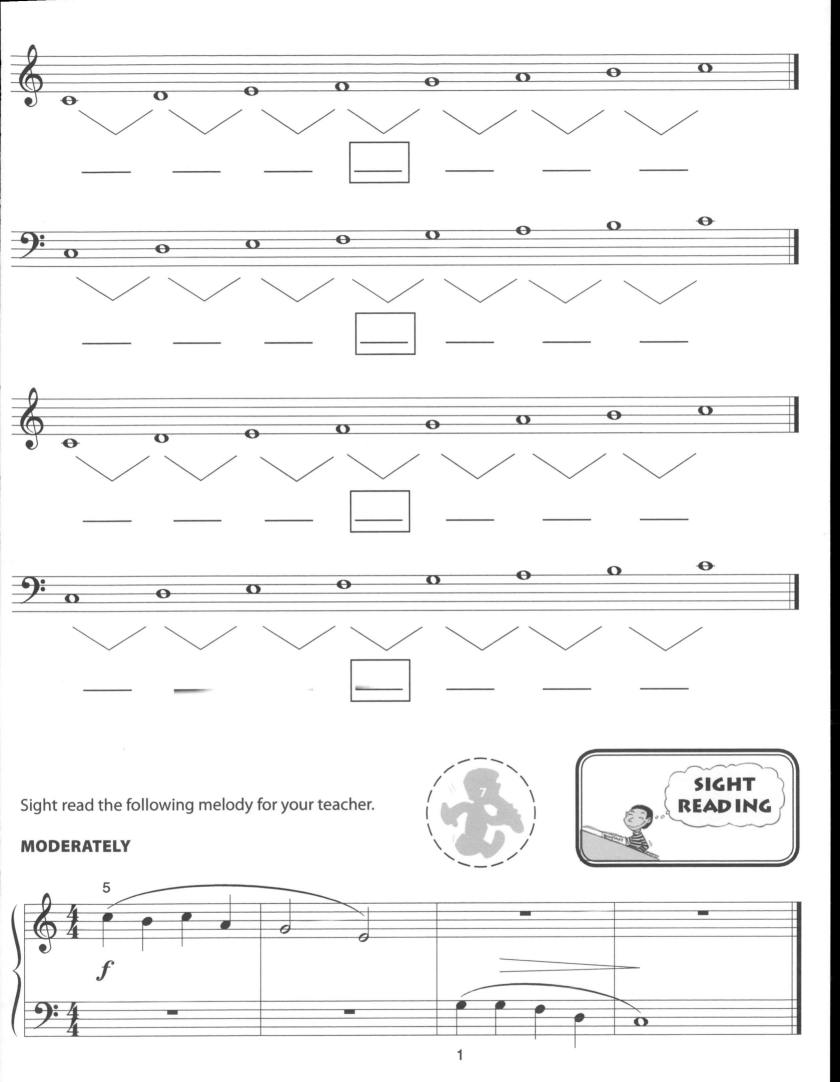

Sight read the following melody for your teacher.

MODERATELY

SIGHT READING

CORRESPONDS WITH PAGES 16 & 17 OF BEANSTALK'S LESSON BOOK 2.

WRITING THE C MAJOR SCALE

THINKING CAP
What connects two tetrachords?

To write the **C MAJOR SCALE**, begin on **C** and write a note on each line and space all the way up to the next **C**.

The notes will be: **C D E F G A B C**

(Since the key signature of C major has no sharps or flats, you will not need to add any sharps or flats to the notes.)

Write the C major scale on each staff below. Spread out your work so that the scale takes up the entire line. Don't forget to check the clef! Mark both tetrachords (⌐‾‾‾‾¬) and both semitones (‿). (The first one has been done for you as an example.)

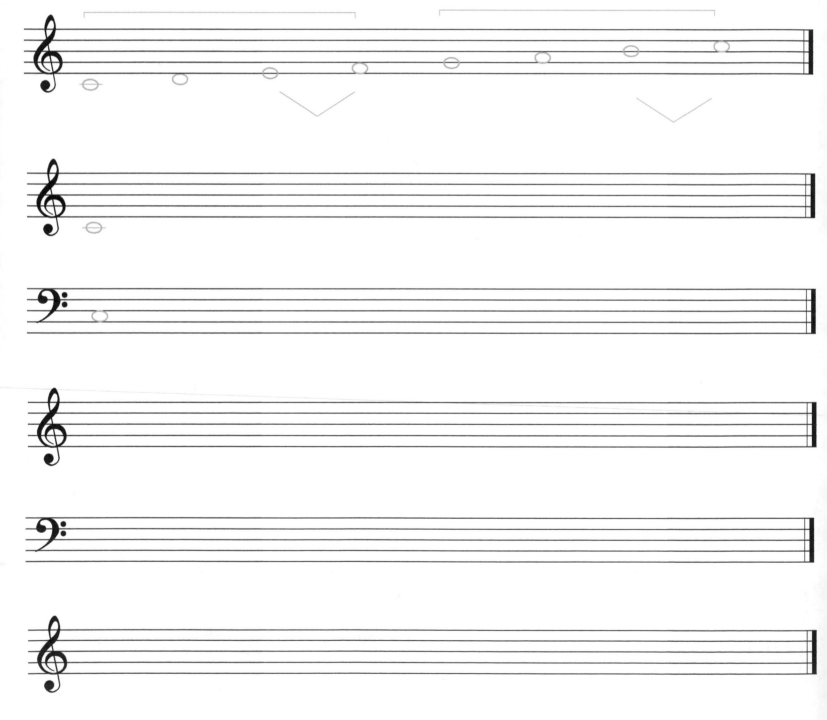

CORRESPONDS WITH PAGE 18 OF BEANSTALK'S LESSON BOOK 2.

C MAJOR TRIAD REVIEW

A C position or C major triad consists of **THREE** notes — **C, E** and **G**. Since there are no sharps or flats in the key of C major, the C major triad does not contain any sharps or flats. Build a C major triad on each of the following C's. (The first one in each clef has been done for you as an example.)

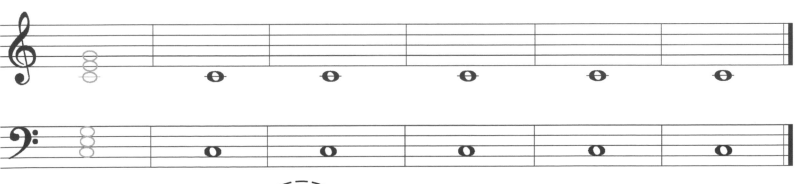

NOW HEAR THIS!

Your teacher will play two short melodies in the key of C major. Close your eyes and listen. After playing each melody twice, your teacher will show you which notes to begin on. Now play the melody.

FOR THE TEACHER:

CORRESPONDS WITH PAGE 18 OF BEANSTALK'S LESSON BOOK 2.

G MAJOR SCALE

THINKING CAP
What note will be a sharp in the key of G major?

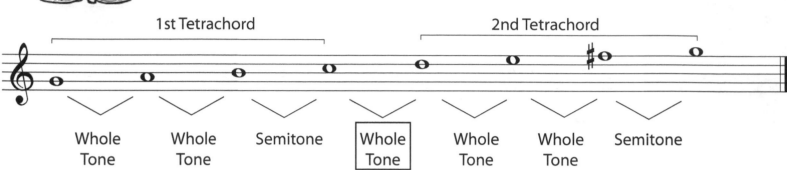

For each of the following G major scales, write **WT** below each **WHOLE TONE** and **ST** below each **SEMITONE**. Mark both tetrachords. (The first one has been done for you as an example.)

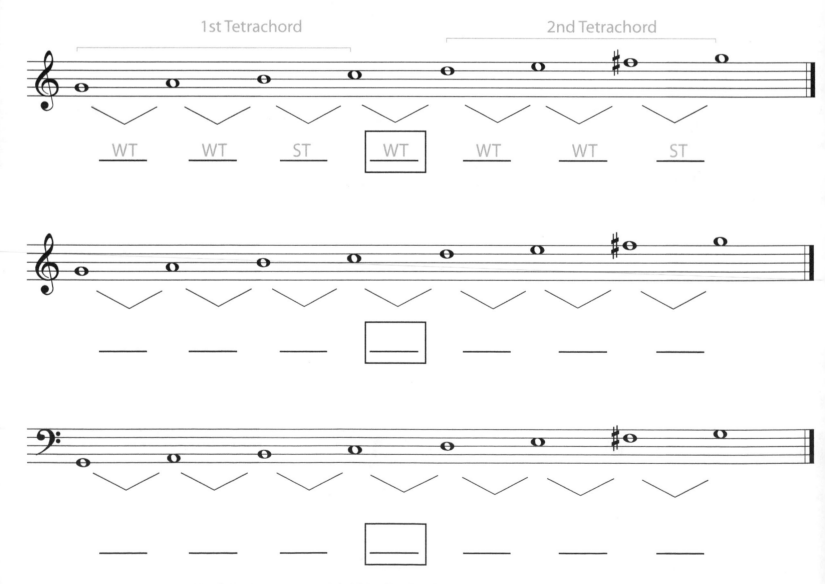

CORRESPONDS WITH PAGES 19 & 20 OF BEANSTALK'S LESSON BOOK 2.

18

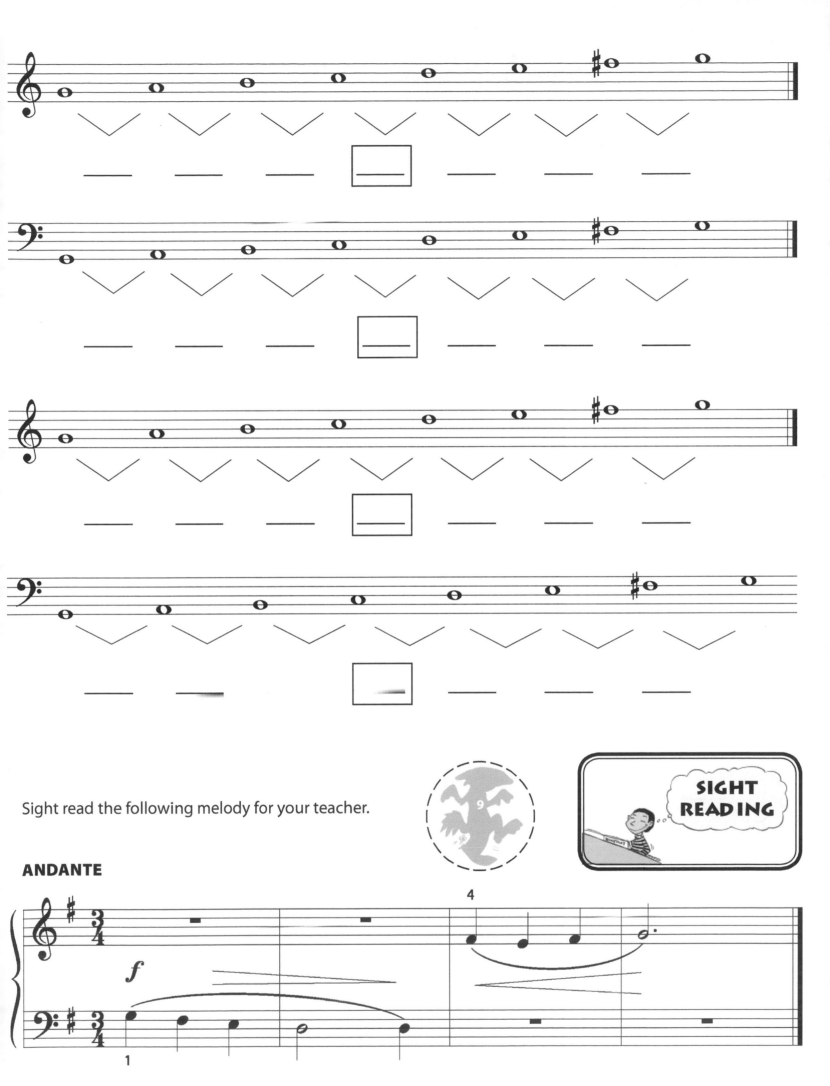

Sight read the following melody for your teacher.

ANDANTE

CORRESPONDS WITH PAGES 19 & 20 OF BEANSTALK'S LESSON BOOK 2.

19

WRITING THE G MAJOR SCALE

To write the G major scale, begin on the G and write a note on each line and space all the way up to the next G.

The notes will be: **G A B C D E F# G**

(Since G major has an **F SHARP** in its key signature, you will need to write a sharp sign in front of the F.)

Write the G major scale on each staff below. Mark both tetrachords (⌐‾‾‾‾⌐) and both semitones (⌣). (The first one has been done for you as an example.)

CORRESPONDS WITH PAGE 21 OF BEANSTALK'S LESSON BOOK 2.

G MAJOR TRIAD REVIEW

A G position or G major triad consists of **THREE** notes — **G, B** and **D**. Although the key of G major contains an **F SHARP**, it does not appear in this triad. Build a G major triad on each of the following G's. (The first one in each clef has been done for you as an example.)

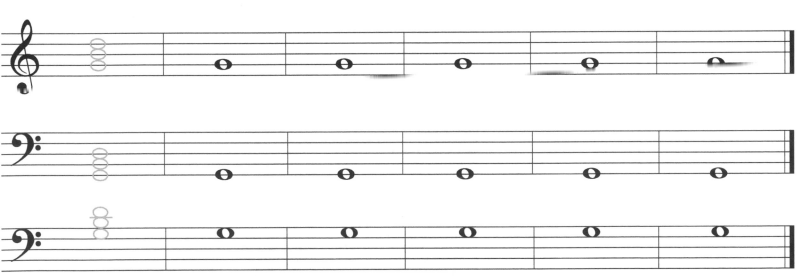

NOW HEAR THIS!

Your teacher will play a series of short melodies in the key of G major. Close your eyes and listen. After having heard the melody played twice, clap the rhythm.

FOR THE TEACHER:

CORRESPONDS WITH PAGE 21 OF BEANSTALK'S LESSON BOOK 2.

F MAJOR SCALE

THINKING CAP

In the key of F major, will the flat go in front of the B or after the B?

1st Tetrachord   2nd Tetrachord

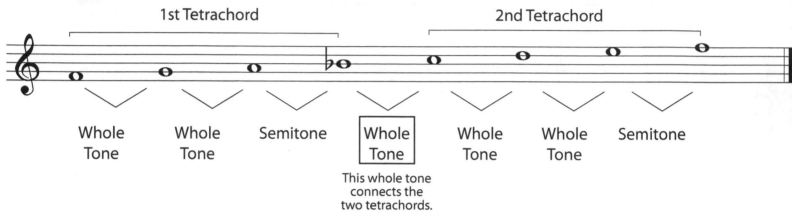

| Whole Tone | Whole Tone | Semitone | Whole Tone | Whole Tone | Whole Tone | Semitone |

This whole tone connects the two tetrachords.

For each of the following F major scales, write **WT** below each **WHOLE TONE** and **ST** below each **SEMITONE**. Mark both tetrachords. (The first one has been done for you as an example.)

1st Tetrachord   2nd Tetrachord

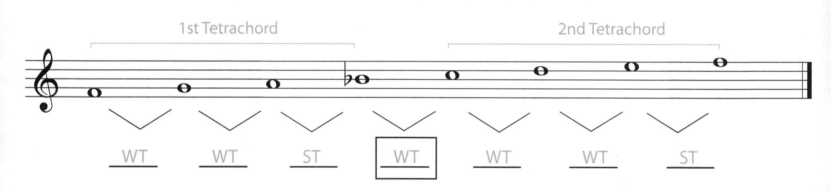

WT   WT   ST   WT   WT   WT   ST

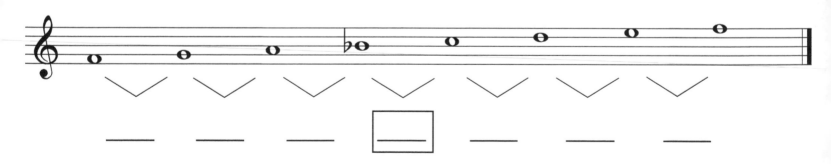

A NEW NOTE

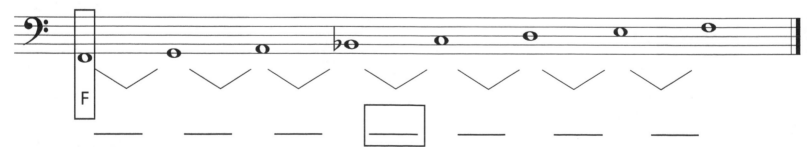

CORRESPONDS WITH PAGES 22 & 23 OF BEANSTALK'S LESSON BOOK 2.

22

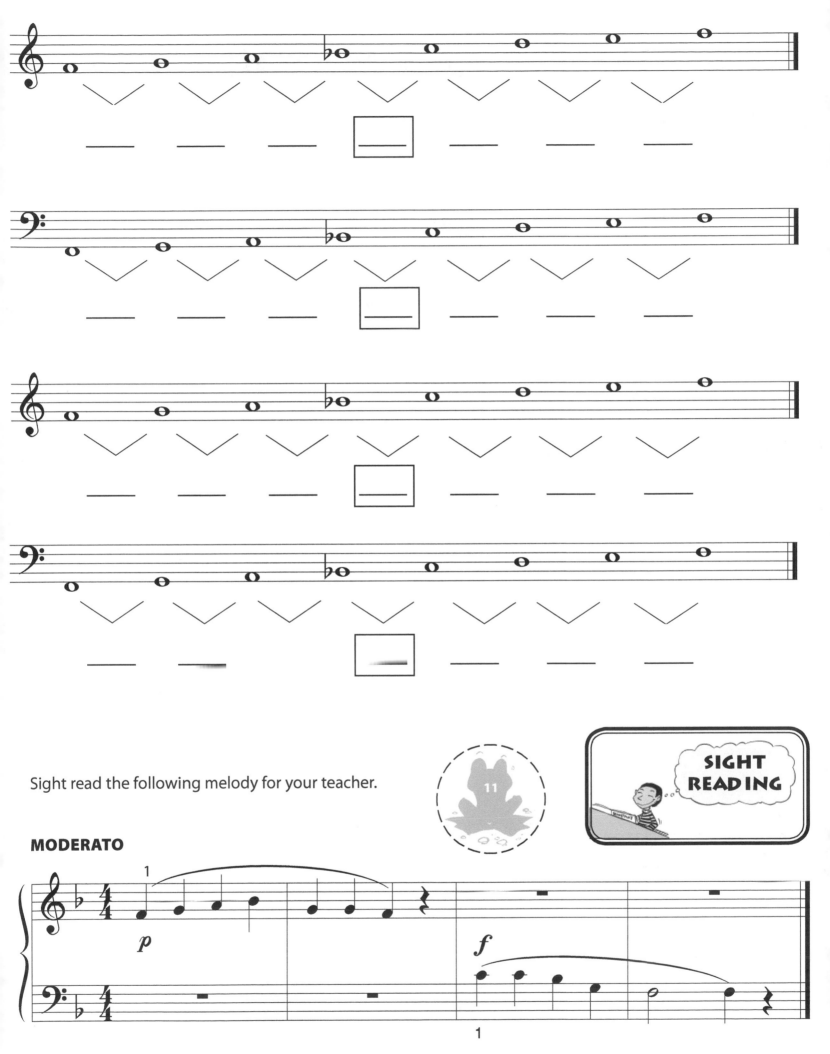

Sight read the following melody for your teacher.

MODERATO

CORRESPONDS WITH PAGES 22 & 23 OF BEANSTALK'S LESSON BOOK 2.

23

WRITING THE F MAJOR SCALE

To write the **F MAJOR SCALE**, begin on F and write a note on each line and space all the way up to the next F.

The notes will be: **F G A B♭ C D E F**

(Since F major has a **B FLAT** in its key signature, you will need to write a flat sign in front of the B.)

Write the F major scale on each staff below. Mark both tetrachords (⌐────────⌐) and both semitones (◡). (The first one has been done for you as an example.)

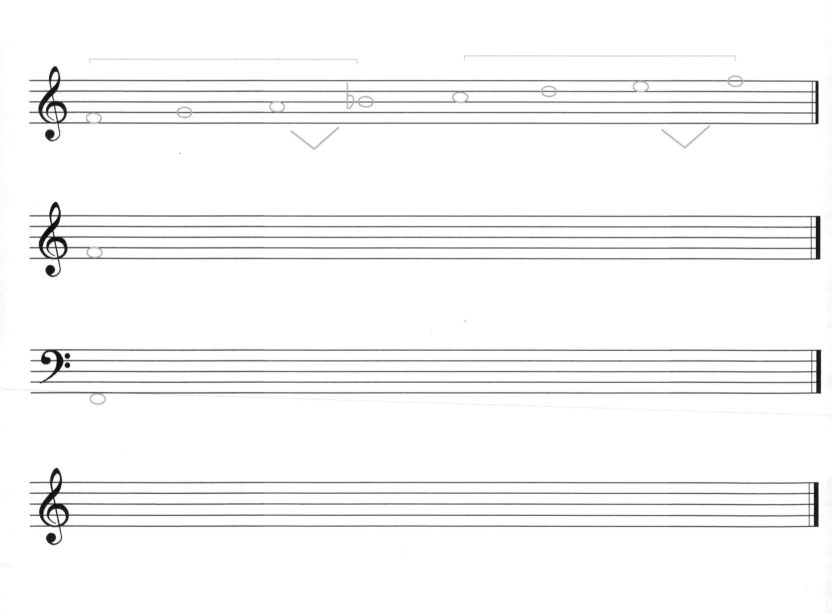

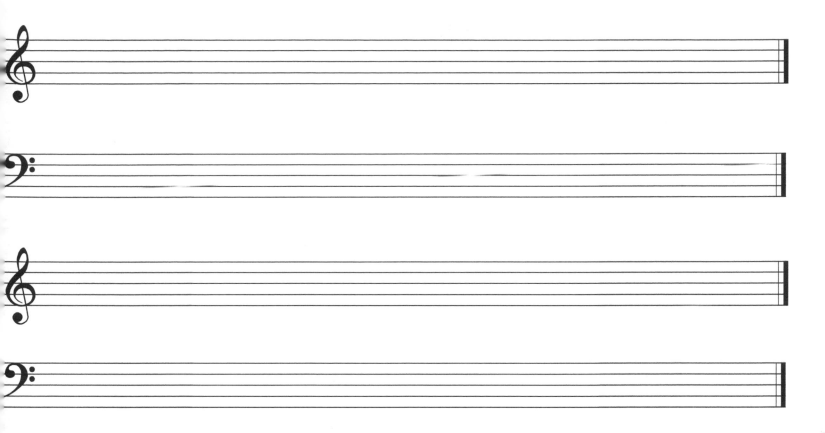

F MAJOR TRIAD REVIEW

An F position or F major triad consists of **THREE** notes — **F, A** and **C.** Although the key of F major contains a **B FLAT**, it does not appear in this triad. Build an F major triad on each of the following F's. (The first one in each clef has been done for you as an example.)

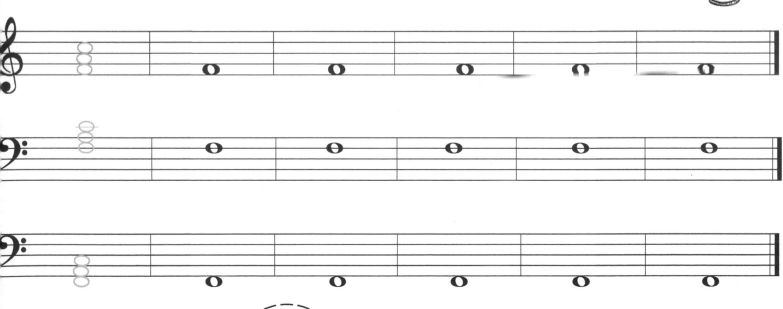

NOW HEAR THIS!
Your teacher will play two short melodies in the key of F major. Close your eyes and listen. After having been shown the note on which to begin, play the melody.

FOR THE TEACHER:

CORRESPONDS WITH PAGE 24 OF BEANSTALK'S LESSON BOOK 2.

REVIEW

13

1. Name the following notes on the grand staff.

2. Write the following notes on the grand staff. Use half notes. (Remember to check the stems.)

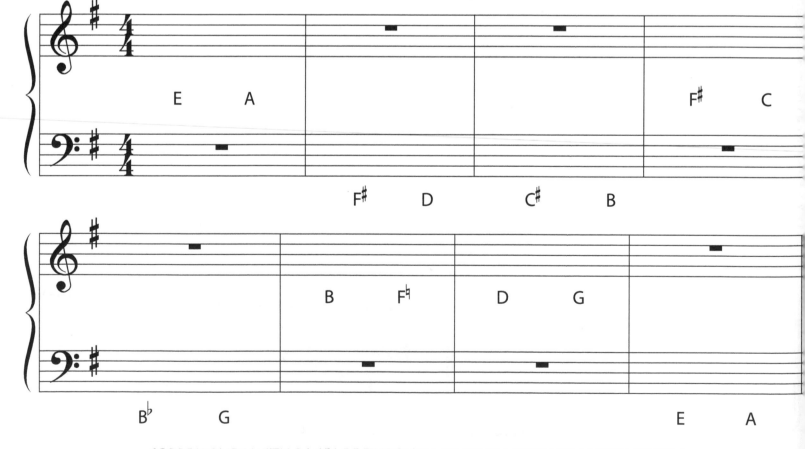

CORRESPONDS WITH PAGES 25 THROUGH 28 OF BEANSTALK'S LESSON BOOK 2.

3. Write the counts and add bar lines to the following. Clap the rhythm and count out loud.

4. Name the following intervals.

_____ _____ _____ _____ _____ _____

5. Complete each of the following **HARMONIC** intervals by adding a note above the given note.

| 5th | 2nd | 6th | 3rd | 7th | 4th |

6. For each key marked by an **X** draw an arrow to the key which is a **SEMITONE** higher.

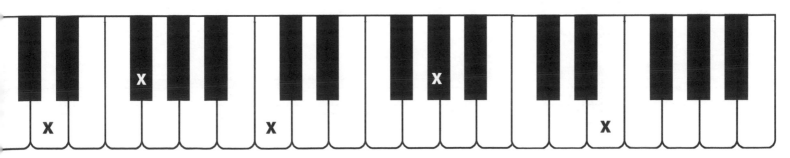

CORRESPONDS WITH PAGES 25 THROUGH 28 OF BEANSTALK'S LESSON BOOK 2.

7. For each key marked by an **X** draw an arrow to the key which is a **WHOLE TONE** lower.

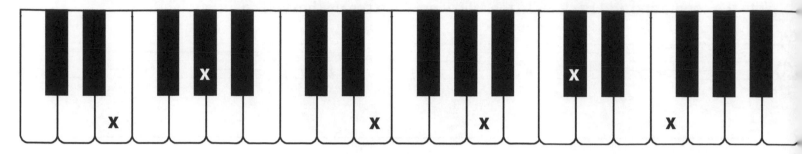

8. Write **WT** below each **WHOLE TONE** and **ST** below each **SEMITONE**. Mark the **TETRACHORDS**.
   Name the **SCALES**.

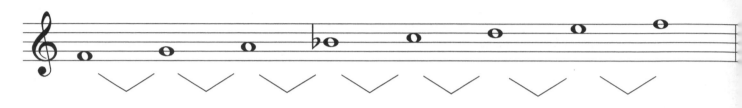

SCALE: ____ ____ ____ ____ ____ ____ ____ ____

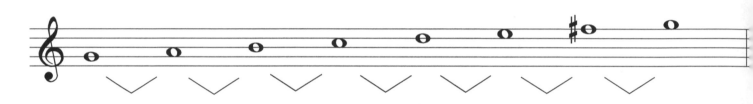

SCALE: ____ ____ ____ ____ ____ ____ ____ ____

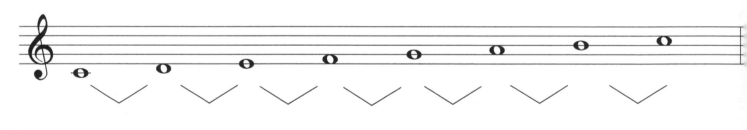

SCALE: ____ ____ ____ ____ ____ ____ ____ ____

9. Complete the following triads using whole notes.

C Major   G Major   F Major

F Major   C Major   G Major   F Major   G Major

CORRESPONDS WITH PAGES 25 THROUGH 28 OF BEANSTALK'S LESSON BOOK 2.

28

10. Write the following scales. Use whole notes.

G Major

C Major

F Major

11. Match each of the following Italian terms to its correct English meaning:

ALLEGRETTO	in a singing style
CANTABILE	gracefully
GRAZIOSO	at a moderate speed
LENTO	gradually slower
RITARDANDO	quickly, but not as quickly as allegro
MODERATO	slowly

NOW HEAR THIS!

1. Your teacher will play a series of intervals once. Answer "harmonic" or "melodic."
2. Your teacher will play a melody in the key of G major twice. Clap the rhythm you hear.
3. Your teacher will play a melody in the key of F major twice. After having been shown the note on which to begin, play the melody.

CORRESPONDS WITH PAGES 25 THROUGH 28 OF BEANSTALK'S LESSON BOOK 2.

PUZZLE FUN!

Color the C major key signature parachute **RED**.
Color the G major key signature parachute **DARK BLUE**.
Color the F major key signature parachute **GREEN**.
Color the C major triad parachute **ORANGE**.

Color the G major triad parachute **PURPLE**.
Color the F major triad parachute **YELLOW**.
Color the C major scale parachute **BROWN**.
Color the G major scale parachute **PINK**.
Color the F major scale parachute **LIGHT BLUE**.

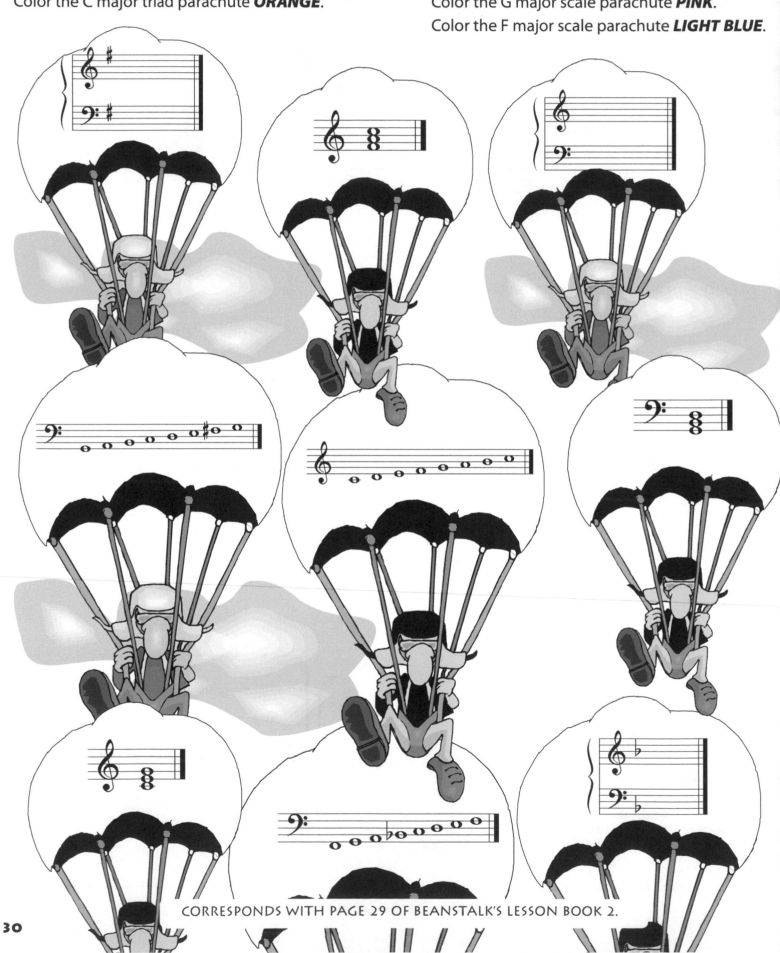

CORRESPONDS WITH PAGE 29 OF BEANSTALK'S LESSON BOOK 2.

COMPOSE IT!

Below you will find **EIGHT** measures. Using the notes of the
G **MAJOR SCALE (G A B C D E F♯ G)**, write your own composition!
Remember that you must have **THREE** beats (or counts)
in each measure. **HAVE FUN**!

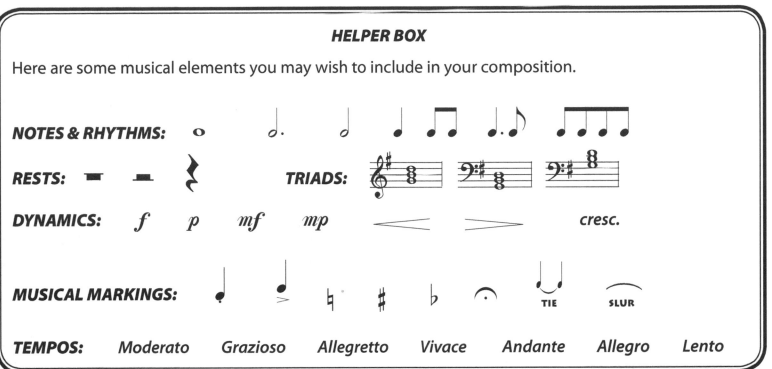

HELPER BOX

Here are some musical elements you may wish to include in your composition.

NOTES & RHYTHMS:

RESTS: **TRIADS:**

DYNAMICS: *f*   *p*   *mf*   *mp*   <   >   cresc.

MUSICAL MARKINGS: ♮   ♯   ♭   TIE   SLUR

TEMPOS: *Moderato*   *Grazioso*   *Allegretto*   *Vivace*   *Andante*   *Allegro*   *Lento*

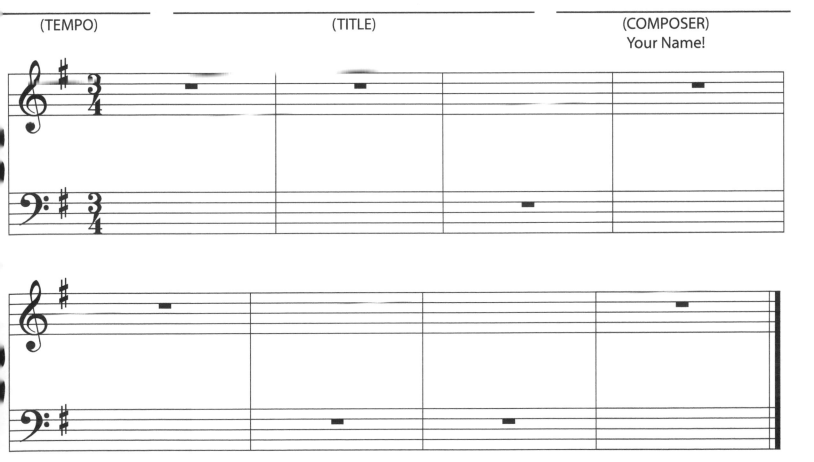

(TEMPO)   (TITLE)   (COMPOSER)
                                  Your Name!

CORRESPONDS WITH PAGE 29 OF BEANSTALK'S LESSON BOOK 2.

D MAJOR SCALE

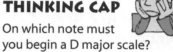

THINKING CAP

On which note must
you begin a D major scale?

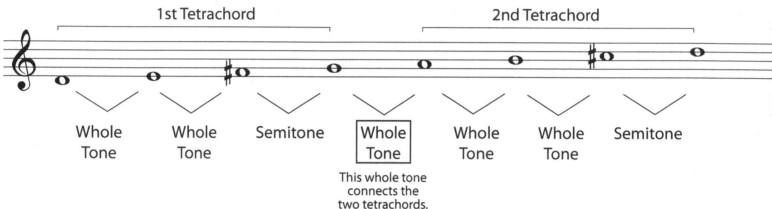

1st Tetrachord   **2nd Tetrachord**

Whole Tone — Whole Tone — Semitone — **Whole Tone** — Whole Tone — Whole Tone — Semitone

This whole tone connects the two tetrachords.

For the following D major scales, write **WT** below each **WHOLE TONE** and **ST** below each **SEMITONE**. Mark both tetrachords. (The first one has been done for you as an example.)

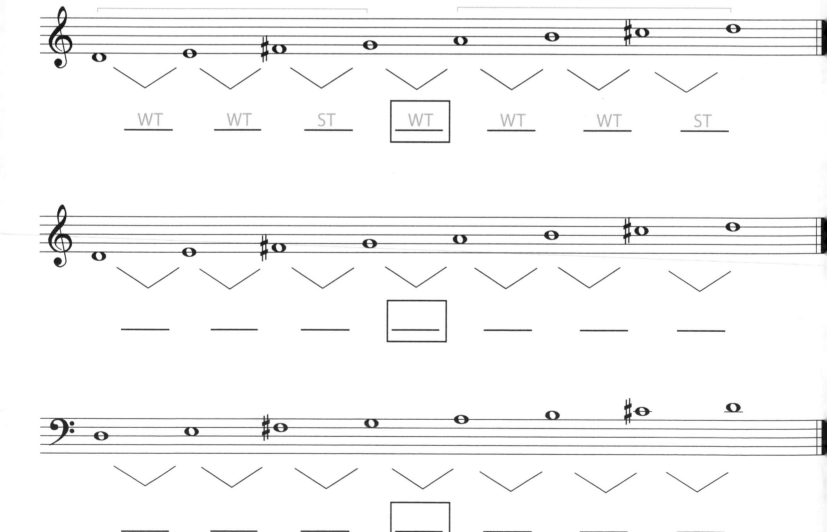

CORRESPONDS WITH PAGES 30 & 31 OF BEANSTALK'S LESSON BOOK 2.

32

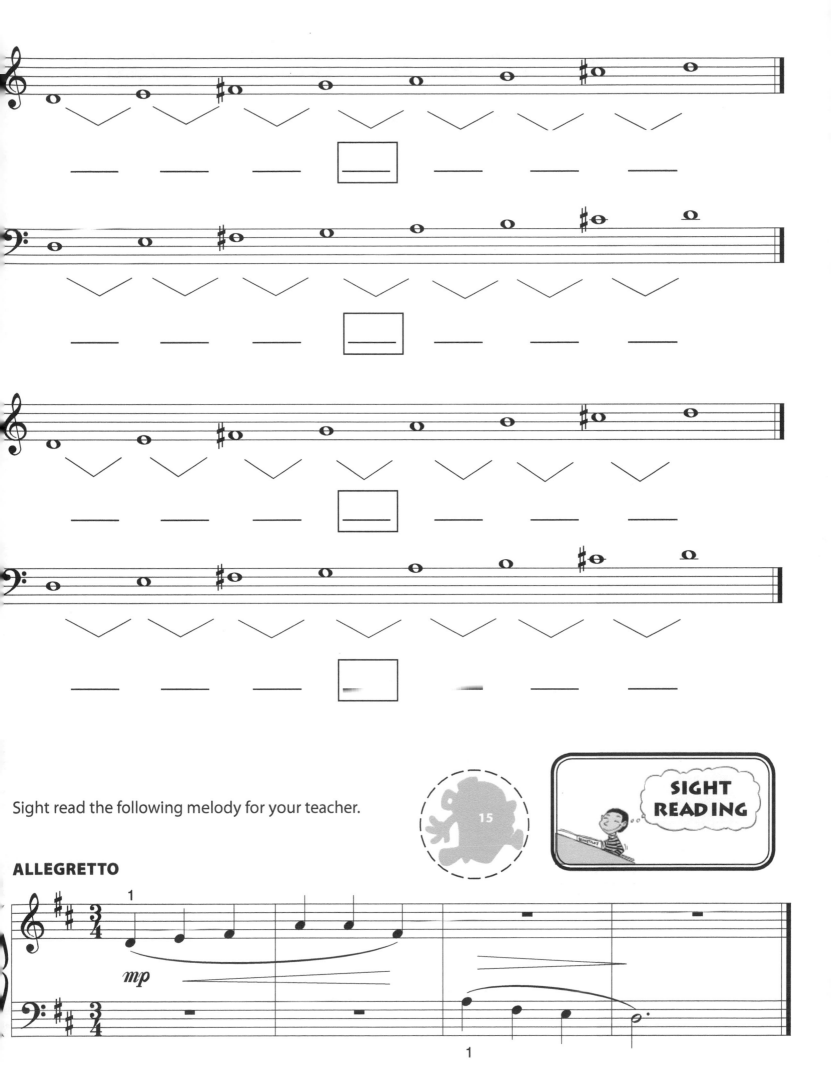

Sight read the following melody for your teacher.

ALLEGRETTO

CORRESPONDS WITH PAGES 30 & 31 OF BEANSTALK'S LESSON BOOK 2.

33

WRITING THE D MAJOR SCALE

To write the **D MAJOR SCALE**, begin on D and write a note on each line and space all the way up to the next D.

The notes will be: **D E F♯ G A B C♯ D**

(Since D major has an F♯ and a C♯ in its key signature, you will need to write a sharp sign in front of the F and C.)

Write the D major scale on each staff below. Mark both tetrachords (⌐———⌐) and both semitones (⌣). (The first one has been done for you as an example.)

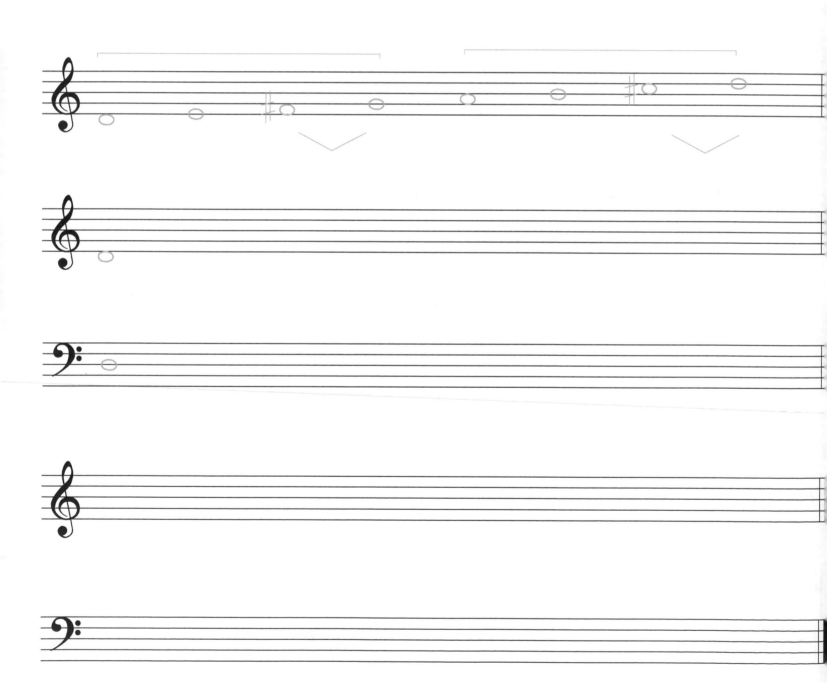

CORRESPONDS WITH PAGE 32 OF BEANSTALK'S LESSON BOOK 2.

D MAJOR TRIAD REVIEW

A D position or D major triad consists of **THREE** notes — **D, F#** and **A**. Since the key signature of D major contains an F# and a C#, it is necessary to put a sharp sign in front of the F. Build a D major triad on each of the following D's. (The first one in each clef has been done for you as an example.)

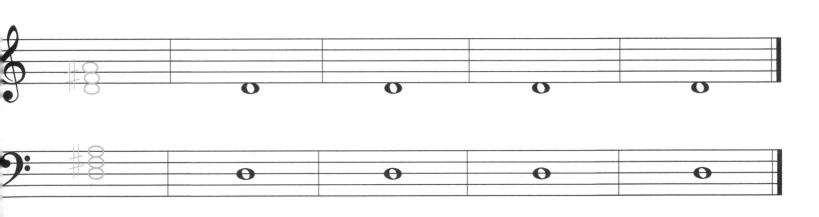

FOR THE TEACHER:

CORRESPONDS WITH PAGE 32 OF BEANSTALK'S LESSON BOOK 2.

LEDGER LINES

Notes that are written above or below the music staff are called **LEDGER LINE** notes.

In the **TREBLE CLEF**, the first three **LEDGER LINE** notes **ABOVE** the staff are:

A   B   C

Name the following ledger line notes.

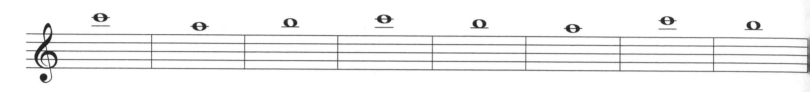

When writing **LEDGER LINE** notes, be sure that none of the lines are too close together or too far apart. Keep the same distance between the lines as exists on the music staff.

Incorrect   Correct

Write the following **LEDGER LINE** notes in the treble clef.

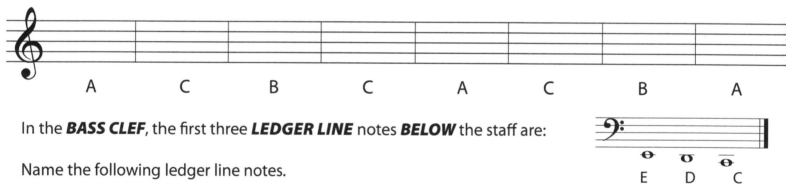

A   C   B   C   A   C   B   A

In the **BASS CLEF**, the first three **LEDGER LINE** notes **BELOW** the staff are:

Name the following ledger line notes.

E   D   C

When writing **LEDGER LINE** notes in the bass clef, it is also important to space your lines correctly:

Incorrect   Correct

Write the following **LEDGER LINE** notes in the bass clef.

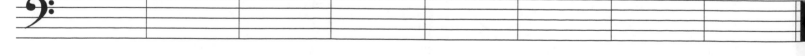

C   E   D   E   C   D   E   C

CORRESPONDS WITH PAGES 33 & 34 OF BEANSTALK'S LESSON BOOK 2.

 TIME SIGNATURE

In $\frac{6}{8}$ time: **6** tells that there are six counts in each measure
8 tells us that each **EIGHTH NOTE** receives **ONE** count

This is a **QUARTER REST**: In $\frac{6}{8}$ time this rest receives **TWO** counts.

Write a **QUARTER REST** in each of the measures below.
Write how many counts each rest receives on the line.

This is an **EIGHTH REST**: In $\frac{6}{8}$ time this rest receives **ONE** count.

Write an **EIGHTH REST** in each of the measures below.
Write how many counts each rest receives on the line.

This is a dotted quarter rest: It is worth three counts in $\frac{6}{8}$ time. While you may occasionally see this, you will most often see the combination of a quarter rest and an eighth rest, also worth three counts. In $\frac{6}{8}$ time, these notes and rests receive the following counts:

♪ or ✼ = 1 count   ♩ or 𝄽 – 2 counts   ♩. or 𝄽. – 3 counts   ♩. or ▬ = 6 counts

For the following notes and rests, write how many counts each receives in $\frac{6}{8}$ time.

Write the counts and add bar lines to the following. Clap the rhythm and count out loud.

1 2 3 4 5 6

CORRESPONDS WITH PAGES 35 THROUGH 37 OF BEANSTALK'S LESSON BOOK 2.

THE A MAJOR SCALE

THINKING CAP
What is the key signature for A major?

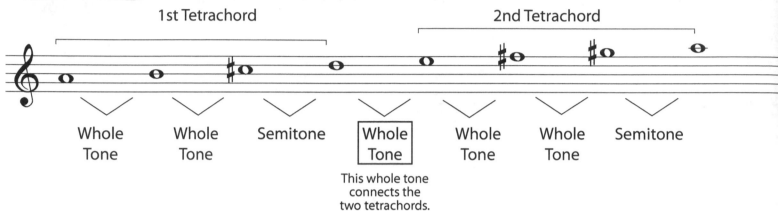

| 1st Tetrachord | | | | 2nd Tetrachord | | |

Whole Tone — Whole Tone — Semitone — **Whole Tone** — Whole Tone — Whole Tone — Semitone

This whole tone connects the two tetrachords.

For the following A major scales, write **WT** below each **WHOLE TONE** and **ST** below each **SEMITONE**. Mark both tetrachords. (The first one has been done for you as an example.)

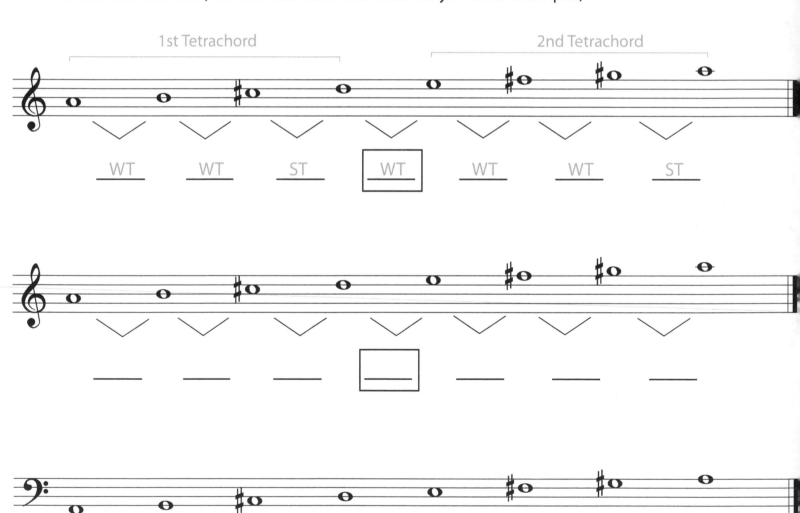

CORRESPONDS WITH PAGES 38 THROUGH 40 OF BEANSTALK'S LESSON BOOK 2.

38

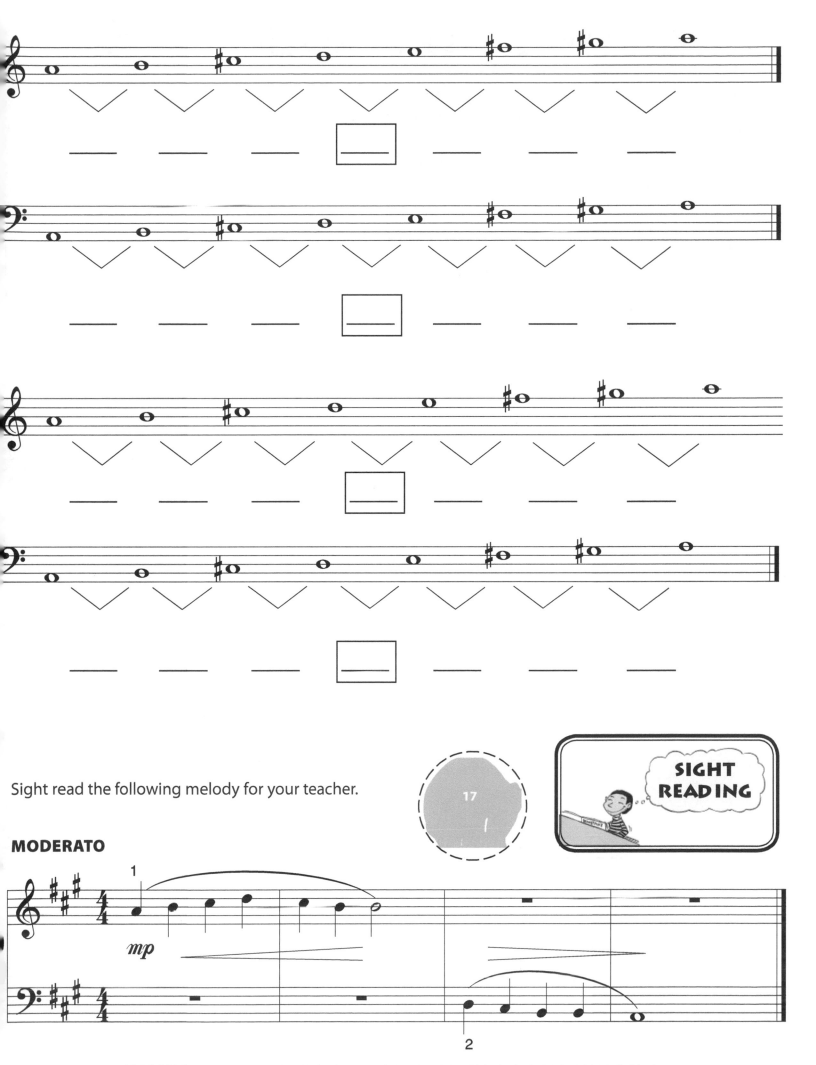

Sight read the following melody for your teacher.

SIGHT READING

MODERATO

CORRESPONDS WITH PAGES 38 THROUGH 40 OF BEANSTALK'S LESSON BOOK 2.

WRITING THE A MAJOR SCALE

To write the **A MAJOR SCALE**, begin on A and write a note on each line and space all the way up to the next A.

The notes will be: **A B C♯ D E F♯ G♯ A**

(Since A major has an F♯, C♯ and a G♯ in its key signature, you will need to write a sharp sign in front of the F, C and G.)

Write the A major scale on each staff below. Mark both tetrachords (⌐────) and both semitones (‿). (The first one has been done for you as an example

CORRESPONDS WITH PAGES 41 & 42 OF BEANSTALK'S LESSON BOOK 2.

THE A MAJOR TRIAD

An A major triad consists of **THREE** notes — **A, C#** and **E**. Since the key signature of A major contains an F#, C# and G#, it is necessary to put a sharp sign in front of the C. Build an A major triad on each of the following A's. (The first one in each clef has been done for you as an example.)

FOR THE TEACHER:

CORRESPONDS WITH PAGES 41 & 42 OF BEANSTALK'S LESSON BOOK 2.

41

TRIPLETS

A triplet is made up of **THREE** notes that are played in the same time as it would normally take to play **TWO**:

Two EIGHTH notes are counted like this: ♪♪ or ♪♪
one and   1 +

A **TRIPLET** is counted like this:
1 a la

COMMON TIME means the same as $\frac{4}{4}$.

Write the counts and add bar lines to the following. Clap the rhythm and count out loud.

NOW HEAR THIS!

Your teacher will play a series of short melodies containing triplets. Close your eyes and listen. After having heard the melody played twice, clap the rhythm.

FOR THE TEACHER:

CORRESPONDS WITH PAGES 43 & 44 OF BEANSTALK'S LESSON BOOK 2.

MORE KEY SIGNATURES!

Practice writing the following **KEY SIGNATURES**. (The first one has been done for you in each case.)

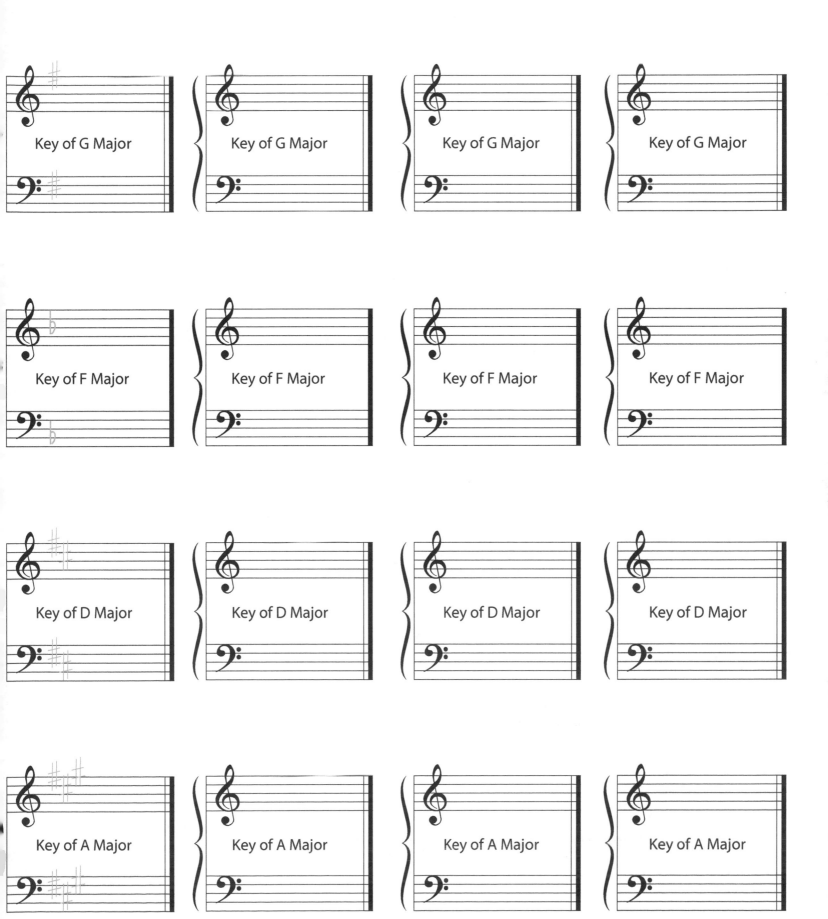

CORRESPONDS WITH PAGES 45 & 46 OF BEANSTALK'S LESSON BOOK 2.

43

PUZZLE FUN!

ITALIAN TERMS

In each box, circle the correct meaning of the Italian term:

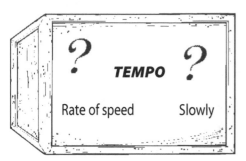

TEMPO

Rate of speed   Slowly

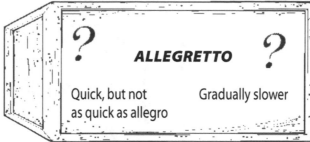

ALLEGRETTO

Quick, but not   Gradually slower
as quick as allegro

ALLEGRO

Quick &   Gracefully
lively

RITARDANDO

Go back to the beginning
and play to FINE

Gradually slower

ANDANTE

Slowly at a   Play at a
walking pace   moderate speed

GRAZIOSO

Gracefully   Slowly

LENTO

In a singing style   Slowly

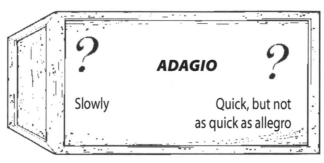

ADAGIO

Slowly   Quick, but not
as quick as allegro

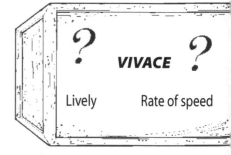

VIVACE

Lively   Rate of speed

DC al FINE

Lively   Go back to the beginning
and play to FINE

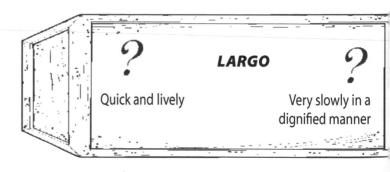

LARGO

Quick and lively   Very slowly in a
dignified manner

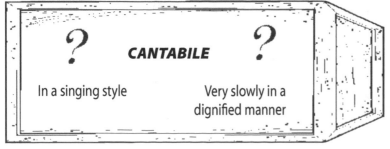

CANTABILE

In a singing style   Very slowly in a
dignified manner

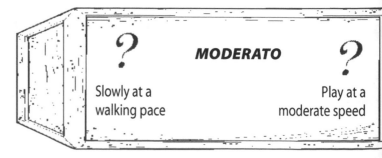

MODERATO

Slowly at a   Play at a
walking pace   moderate speed

CORRESPONDS WITH PAGE 47 OF BEANSTALK'S LESSON BOOK 2.

INTRODUCING 8THS OR OCTAVES

An interval of an 8th (octave) is written **LINE** to **SPACE** or **SPACE** to **LINE**:

THINKING CAP
What note would be an 8th higher than E Flat?

For each of the following, write the note that is an 8th (octave) **ABOVE**. Use whole notes.

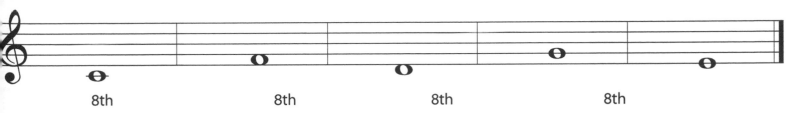

8th   8th   8th   8th

For each of the following, write the note that is an 8th (octave) **BELOW**. Use whole notes.

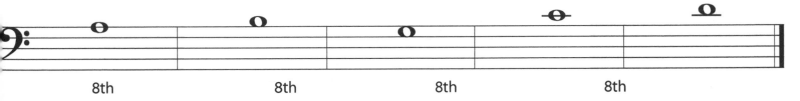

8th   8th   8th   8th

DYNAMICS

Dynamic signs tell us how loud or soft to play.

NEW!   *pp* or **PIANISSIMO** tells us to play **VERY SOFTLY**.
            ff or **FORTISSIMO** tells us to play **VERY LOUDLY**.

Match the following dynamic markings to their correct meanings by drawing a line.

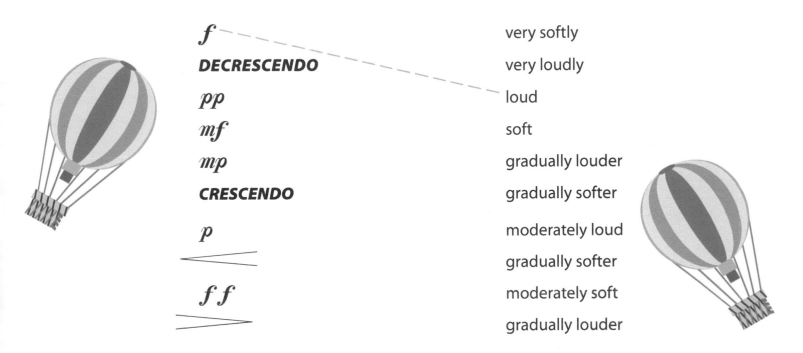

f	very softly
DECRESCENDO	very loudly
pp	loud
mf	soft
mp	gradually louder
CRESCENDO	gradually softer
p	moderately loud
<	gradually softer
ff	moderately soft
>	gradually louder

CORRESPONDS WITH PAGES 48 & 49 OF BEANSTALK'S LESSON BOOK 2.

REVIEW

1. Name the following notes on the grand staff.

2. Write the following **LEDGER LINE** notes on the grand staff. Use quarter notes. (Remember to check the stems.)

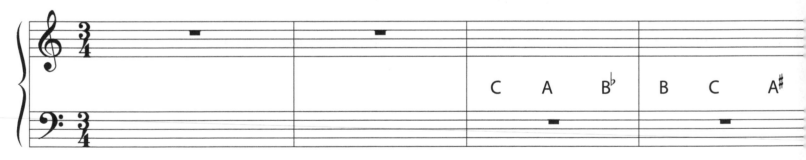

| C | A | B♭ | B | C | A♯ |

E   C   D   C   E♭   D

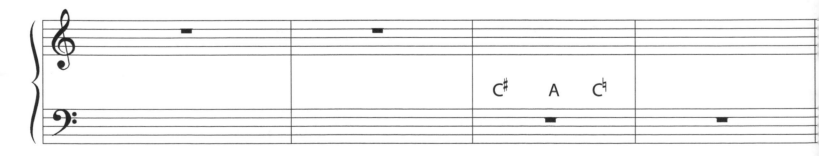

| C♯ | A | C♮ |

E   C♯   D   C   B♭   E

CORRESPONDS WITH PAGE 50 OF BEANSTALK'S LESSON BOOK 2.

3. Write the counts and add bar lines to the following. Clap the rhythm and count out loud.

4. Complete each of the following **HARMONIC** intervals by adding a note above the given note. Use whole notes.

3rd   5th   7th   2nd   4th   8th   6th

5. Name the following intervals.

6. Write the following triads. Use whole notes.

C major   G major   F major   D major   A major

C major   G major   F major   D major   A major
                 (High and Low)   (High and Low)

CORRESPONDS WITH PAGE 50 OF BEANSTALK'S LESSON BOOK 2.

7. For each key marked by an **X**, draw an arrow to the key that is a **SEMITONE** lower.

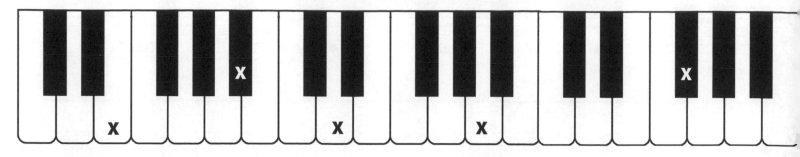

8. For each key marked by an X, draw an arrow to the key that is a **WHOLE TONE** higher.

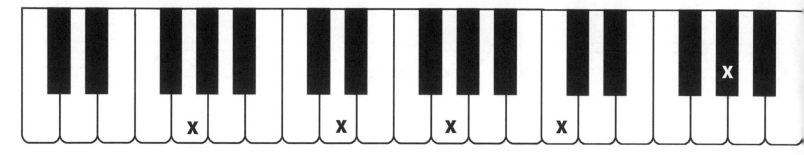

9 . Write the following scales. Use whole notes.

C major

G major

F major

D major

A major

CORRESPONDS WITH PAGE 50 OF BEANSTALK'S LESSON BOOK 2.